Sitting On a Rock, Thinking

Essays

Sharon Slaton Howell

Black Wolf Press
2011

Printed in the USA

Published by:
Black Wolf Press
1800 Grand Avenue
Knoxville, Tennessee 37916

Printed and bound in the United States of America.

2nd Printing

Library of Congress Control Number: 2011918501

ISBN-13: 978-0-615-55379-5

ISBN-10: 0-615-55379-6

Table of Contents

Celebrating Autumn

My favorite season of them all. How do I enjoy
September, October and November? By:

* * *decorating our front porch with chrysanthemums, usually
in shades of yellow and gold and rust, sometimes wine. Of course,
I have to add just the right pumpkins. I check them out at the
roadside stands as though they're going to be permanent, so
important is it to get just the right shape and size, with a stem that
curls just so and has a touch of green on it. And always now that I
have him, I put out Cletus, our harvest figure. He's the cutest little
fellow, about 3 feet high, with a farmer's cover-alls, plaid shirt, straw
hat, and happy expression on his face. When I found him at our
neighborhood market some years ago, just knew he was the one
I had to take home. Asked a friend who grew up here in Tennessee,
"What's a good Southern name for a farmer?" She thought for awhile,
and came back with Cletus.

* * *taking a drive through the countryside, exploring back
roads, to see pumpkins in mist -- so very picturesque, pure poetry
to me.

* * *eating crisp apples and cinnamon donuts. I've even
added yummy hot chocolate with lots of whipped cream over at
a local café, imbibed outside early on chilly mornings. My
favorite spot is a table at one corner of the building where the cold
winds come whistling around.

* * * reveling in autumn leaves. I make angels in the leaves on
our neighbor's hill (yes, I do this); standing outside when leaves are
pelting down just like I'm standing under a rain shower, delighting

as they land in my. hair; rolling in a pile of just-raked leaves with one of our dogs who gets a kick out of messing everything up.

* * * sleeping with the windows open. (Is there anything quite like non-air conditioned air?)

* * *taking the time to watch October's mellow golden sun stream through wind-rippled branches and perform a ballet across rug, bookcase, and wall-- one of nature's many magic shows.

* * *in order to have our yard light up come spring, planting dozens of daffodils, putting in pretty-faced pansies.

You fellow autumn-aficiandos no doubt have your own rituals to celebrate this season, but these are some of mine.

On Writing

When engaged in work of a literary persuasion, sometimes creations show up at my mental door fully clothed. At other times, at the completion of one of these rascals, I feel I've just run a marathon (or tried to).

But however writing comes --easy, or labored--like it was for Flaubert (so they say) who took all one morning to put a comma in, and all afternoon to take it out, there are few things in my book that can compare to some piece of writing that is "there". When words have established themselves, and there's no more to be shared on a certain topic, insight or conviction, at least at that particular time -what a feeling this is.

It has been my experience that writers have so little say in whether they compose or not. Thoughts begin to flow, words are set to go, and inspiration must be attended to with singleness of heart. Then and there.

Those who do this gathering of ideas from above, inhabit a universe they're in, but all too often not of--sensitive beings who dwell apart.

So give them, world, consideration kind.

You are richer far

for writers being as they are.

A Nice Place to Be

We never expected to see the amazing creativity of the people down here. (I say "down" being that we came from Boston). Such diverse talent! Behind every rock and tree, it almost seems, one is delighted to find an artist of some kind--sculptor, photographer, painter, writer, poet, musician, craftsman--folks simply doing what they were born to do. Or those who get an idea, and just go out and do it. As one native Tennessean once said to us, no one ever told them they couldn't.

How can one state have so many with such ability? Perhaps it's the air, or the water. Or the gorgeous scenery. Speaking of which, two aspects of Tennessee's beauty I particularly like are the ways the skies look after the rain has stopped, and the sun comes shining through. One can almost hear the Hallelujah chorus as the light comes streaming down.

Then there's the autumn. Not as calendar-vivid as the ones we knew in New England, especially Vermont. But lovely enough to enjoy thoroughly. In September, I've noticed that the woods show softening light, the sun making slanted rays. Pumpkins begin to appear in the stores and roadside stands. A few colored leaves make their debut.

Then October, which is my very favorite month of all, the woods though still showing green, become golden. Windows can be left open at night. Leaves with stunning variation--yellow, red, orange, wine--deck out the trees.

Then November with frost likely on morning grass, wood smoke in the air, already too cold for some, but just right for me.

Anyway, if all this wasn't enough, added to all the productivity and natural beauty, there's the warmth and hospitality Southerners are noted for. When all is said, Tennessee is sure one nice place to be.

It's Raining

Maybe it was growing up in hot dry ol' Texas, maybe I'm just one of those persons who like being out in the rain. But what I think accounts for my delight with it is the drought year after year we've experienced here in the South.

I recall two summers especially when my continuing worry was: how are the trees in our woods going to survive this? Blazing sun and not a drop of moisture was taking its toll, not just on them, but on me as well. Then the weather pattern changed, and the rains finally came. Buckets of life-giving rain. Cracks in the ground closed up, the grass turned green, our creek filled up, and all was well again.

What fun it is to sit on our garden bench under a canopy of trees listening to the drops hitting the leaves; walking out alone in the rain when the sky turns to night and street lamps come on--the raindrops glistening on dark green leaves; splashing in puddles just like a kid; getting wrapped up in a downy comforter with a good book, listening to rain hit the roof; going outside after the rain has stopped and looking at the droplets hanging off ends of branches. They look like diamonds to me--diamonds from the sky.

In short, seeing lightning, hearing thunder, then going to my window and getting to exclaim, "It's raining!

To Keep Love Flowing

We who follow Christ, who reverence the Name, can't allow the shame of feeling indifferent to others, wherever in this world they may be. I hope this fellow traveler is learning that when loving others starts to slip, it's more than a blip on the divine screen: it's deadly serious and needs to be gotten at as quickly as possible.

The worse thing about such blatant disobedience to what Jesus taught? A sense of estrangement from God -- not that He ever stops caring about us. But our Father who is all Love is not going to follow us out the door while we indulge in a little hate! Do we want to lose the look of approval on His face?

Something else our Master taught has helped me more than once when I needed to regain my right mind, so to speak. When feeling unloving toward others. It's where Jesus says that the Father sends rain on the just and unjust. In other words, no one is excluded from His blessings. This is from the Sermon the Mount, as many of you will recognize.

If nothing else, a concern for our own well-being should impel a return to Him before it's too late. How many diseases can be traced to a lack of love felt and expressed, a Canadian friend once wrote -- Samuel Greenwood, whose essays have led me to heaven's door.

With the armor of the Word, and no fooling-praying ,this need not be the case. I John puts it clearly: "God is love; and he that dwelleth in love, dwelleth in God and God in him."

Walking Down Huntington Avenue
(Boston, Massachusetts)

That angels can take the form of men, I can attest, for one day such a Being walked along with me. It was some years ago now, but as real and tangible as you are, dear reader.

Whether male or female, I couldn't say. But immensely tall and powerful it was--yet so gentle and reassuring. And what others have reported about that dazzling white is true. For its garment I could see out of the corner of my eye behind my left shoulder as the angel accompanied me. This was the whitest white I had ever seen.

What did it mean? Was I in danger of some kind? I still do not know. But one day perhaps I shall. But that angels do appear as men I feel is indisputably true.

Angels looked after Jesus. And they take care of me and you.

("For he shall give his angels charge over thee, to keep thee in all thy ways." 91 st Psalm)

Childlike

The scene from my office window that day might be seen every day someplace in the world; a puppy jumping all over a delighted little boy. But so heartwarming was this picture that it left a vivid impression on me. The sheer joy of living, the warmth and affection the puppy and the little boy were radiating, reached right across the street to me.

Life's responsibilities were resting heavily on me at this time, and this tender exchange lifted me right up mentally. And spiritually.

I say "spiritually" because I couldn't help thinking of something Christ Jesus said to his disciples. They had come to him with the question of who would be the greatest in the kingdom of heaven. In response, Jesus called a little child to him, and declared, "Verily I say unto you, Except ye be converted, and become as little children, ye shall not enter into the kingdom of heaven" (Matthew 18:3).

If Jesus recommended childlikeness to us, and felt it to be of critical importance, we know it is a God-given requirement and it's for our own good. Such qualities as innocence, trustfulness, receptivity to good, teachableness, and obedience to our heavenly Father can be expressed by every last one of us.

Our Sherlock Holmes Street Lamp

This is what I think of when gazing at the street lamp at the corner of our driveway. When we lived in New England, there was the most quaint Victorian-looking street lamp in our neighborhood. But it was a long way down our street to see it. A neighbor's sweet dog, Myra, used to love accompanying me on my walks.

My imagination was fired then because of a visit we made to England to take in London's sights--among them 221B Baker Street of Sherlock Holmes fame. Long a fan of Sir Arthur Conan Doyle's stories about the great detective, we just had to visit where we were sure Holmes and Watson were still dwelling. We could almost hear, "The game's afoot!", and see them coming out of the doorway in pursuit of a criminal.

Now, instead of having to walk a long way, I can look out of my office window and see our charming Victorian-era light fixture, shedding a soft, beautiful glow over the landscape. And picture myself back in earlier times.

"Why, income is within"

This was said to me when I was about to depart from a steady paycheck to the uncertainties of self-employment. I had expressed to a friend the fear that was overwhelming me.

Was his remark just so many airy words? No, not at all. This friend, a former Hollywood film director had heard the call to enter Christian work full-time and had proved his statement in spades. With two children in college, no less, and only one means of support which remained to be seen. His intent was to bless, to turn my thoughts to what Christ Jesus taught--that the kingdom of God is within us.

My friend also reminded me of something else Jesus said: "Fear not, little flock; for it is your Father's good pleasure to give you the kingdom."(Luke12:32)

Nevertheless, was I still scared? You bet. And yet, take it from me, all you who believe our Master meant what he said. You can discover as I have that our heavenly Father has countless ways to meet our needs, that despite some dark days we belong to God Who always sees us through when we take to heart what Jesus taught.

What is it About Scotland?

As a happy individual who is usually contented with where I happen to be, there are places I especially treasure. And at the top of this list is Scotland.

Why is this? I cannot tell you. Is it the many illustrious men and women who have done their country proud? Perhaps it's the Scottish people I have met here in Tennessee. No, I think it has to be the sheer beauty of the place. What stunning scenery I have seen!

To go back to the historic figures that have changed my life (yes, they have), first there is William Wallace. I happened to see a documentary about the life of this national hero. I was electrified by the courage of this single man to stand alone for freedom for beloved Scotland. There is no mystery why William Wallace is so revered far and wide.

Then there is Andrew Carnegie, whose vast giving to establish public libraries so that the poorest among us could read for free, inspired me greatly. I owe my love for these public institutions to the charitable work this philanthropist did, all across the globe. How many men, women, and children have been blessed by his unselfish endeavors.

I mentioned the Scots I have personally known. One stands out. --a lovely woman who became employed at a large care facility in Boston, Massachusetts when I was one of the trustees. She had been a manager of· a hotel in Edinburgh, and observing the gracious, efficient way she conducted her duties at her new post, I couldn't help but be impressed. We were fortunate to have her running the show.

A long-time resident of East Tennessee told me that this area was settled largely by Scots, and each year there are Scottish Festivals throughout my state. Those of Scottish ancestry attend in large numbers, and there special food and exciting games can be enjoyed all. These events are open to the public.

Last but certainly not least, it's Scotland's natural beauty that has captured me so: wind-blown grasses, rocky hills, stepping stones in crystal streams, picturesque bridges, stone walls old, castles, ancient oaks dappled in golden light, carpets of brightly-colored leaves in autumn, daffodils gracing churchyard and meadow. And yes, even rain galore.

All this and more is what makes me say, I am sold on Scotland.

Love at First Hold

Great literature and music through the ages have waxed eloquently on the experience of love at first sight. But for me, with our very first pet, it was love at first hold.

There we were at the pet store getting treats for some neighbors' dogs when we happened to wander over to an area where there were some dogs. A couple were on some newspapers in a wire enclosure, and there was this tiny, probably 8-week old black velvet bundle of fur. His eyes were closed, and there was a feisty Chow trying to play with what would be our doggie.

I picked up this little fellow and bingo, fell head over heels in love. My husband was watching this, and after some time of no doubt seeing the rapturous look on my face--can't begin to describe what I was feeling at that moment--got out his checkbook and said, "Well, I guess we're taking this one home."

As anyone knows who has fallen in love with an animal, it's an experience that borders on the divine. Words fail when one tries to capture the feeling. But people's faces say all that needs to be said on the subject. Isn't love grand.

Sitting on a Rock, Thinking

It was the perfect spot where I could go and be alone and think. A not-yet-developed area near our house, with big rocks strewn here and there. My favorite was a huge boulder on a hill that took some work to climb. But the view was worth it.

What was I thinking about then? About writing a book. While being published in magazines and newspapers for many years, my real aspiration was to put out a book.

Lo and behold, this did come to pass. In addition to wanting to be an author of a book, or books, was a desire to have them in free public libraries. Growing up in Dallas, Texas, I was a regular user of our local library, where I would bring home as many books as they'd let me check out. My parents couldn't afford to buy me books. Moreover in later years, I had benefited from my time spent in many of these institutions, especially the world-class Boston Public Library. One day the thought occurred, wouldn't it be exciting to have a book of mine on library shelves some day.

And beyond my wildest, not only are my books in libraries all across the USA, but they're in these places as well. Some of the foreign (to me) spots on the globe that I've heard from:

Santiago, Chile
Dorado, Puerto Rico
Leicester, England
Lyon, France
Okinawa, Japan
Stirling, Scotland
Newcastle, Australia
Bucharest, Romania
Riga, Latvia
Macao, China
Noumea, New Caledonia
Port Adelaide, Australia
Vaduz, Liechtenstein
Wenjiang, China
Malaysia
Hiroshima, Japan
London, England
Blagoevgrad, Bulgaria
Rotterdam, the Netherlands
Osaka, Japan
Halifax, Nova Scotia
Seoul, Korea
Cork, Ireland
Valleta, Malta
Aberystwyth, Wales
Katowice, Poland
Orkney Islands, Scotland
Inverclyde, Scotland
Isle of Man
Warsaw, Poland
Cardiff, Wales
Budapest, Hungary
Saskatchewan, Canada
Tokyo, Japan

Lincoln, England
Canberra, Australia
Glasgow, Scotland
Dunedin, New Zealand
Newfoundland, Canada
Hangzhou, China
Thessalonika, Greece
Guadalajara, Mexico
Livingston, Scotland
Liverpool, England
Alexandria, Egypt
Tallin, Estonia
Yerevan, Armenia
Nagasaki, Japan
Copenhagen, Denmark
Prague, Czech Republic
Barcelona, Spain
Wellington, New Zealand
Colombo, Sri Lanka
Ontario, Canada
Clackmanshire, Scotland
Aberdeen, Scotland
Rekyavik, Iceland
Dublane, Scotland
Hong Kong, China
Pusan, Korea
Paris, France
Devon, England
San Juan, Puerto Rico
Dundee, Scotland
Ottawa, Canada
Nicosia, Cypress
Fife, Scotland
Manilla, the Philippines

Lisbon, Portugal
Raratonga, Cook Islands
Edinburgh, Scotland
Windhoek, Namibia
Cymru, Wales
Buenos Aires, Argentina
Beijing, China
Ballerup, Denmark
Shanghai, China
Thimpu, Kingdom of Bhutan
Queensland, Australia
Sao Paulo, Brazil
Hamilton, Scotland
Bogota, Colombia
Islamabad, Pakistan
Tblisi, Georgia
Inverness, Scotland
Limerick, Ireland
Bridgetown, Barbados
Nanjing, China
Kintilloch, Scotland
Hamilton, New Zealand
Goa, India

Hagatna, Guam
Vienna, Austria
Singapore
Belfast, Northern Ireland
Nara, Japan
Tauranga, New Zealand
Brasov, Romania
Vilnius, Lithuania
Hastings, New Zealand
Brisbane, Australia
Minsk, Belarus
Moscow, Russia
Trieste, Italy
Swaziland, Africa
Kiev, Ukraine
Malmo, Sweden
Limassol, Cypress
Chennai, India
Galway, Ireland
Swansea, Wales
Regina, Canada
Bangor, Northern Ireland
Dumferline, Scotland

Talk about your expanding horizons!

And Angels Smile

My husband comes home from the pet food store with tears in his eyes. "A pitiful little dog is at the adoption center, and desperately needs some love", he tells me. Not thinking about getting another dog, his words hang in the air. But not too long after, I drive over to the store to take a look.

There the dog is, dirty, almost starved, shaking with fear--the light of hope nearly gone from her eyes. (Her former owner or owners, they think, left her by the side of the road to die, which she almost did. Not to mention, she had obviously had, no care whatsoever.) I pick her up gently, cradle her in my lap, and begin filling out adoption forms.

And angels smile.

The young man who helped me with the paper work, asks with moist eyes, "May I carry her to your car?", so glad someone was taking her home, as she probably had only a few more days of life left.

This little trooper, so thin she can scarcely stand up, amazes us by actually climbing our back stairs to look around her new home. A careful, warm, soapy cleaning comes next, then a bit of food for her. That night, I decide to make her a little bed by my side of the bed, in case she needs comforting in the night. Several old blankets piled up, covered over with a soft, clean sheet does the job, for the best night's sleep this little girl has probably had. There's a special glow in the air that surrounds us all.

And angels smile.

Solitude

How one can prefer society's noise to solitude's tranquility is more than the true lover of nature can comprehend. For how can such infinite beauty as our heavenly Father spreads before us be adequately appreciated while in a crowd of people, talking when they have nothing to say -- individuals who just go on and on and never know when to end!

It's indisputable (at least it is to me): contemplating nature and garrulity are incompatible. On forays into the wild, give me a soulful quiet. And possibly a companion (or two or three of the four-legged and furry kind) who know the value of silence.

I love being out in the woods or a forest when winter is past. When mother nature gets out her spring dress, how many shades of green there have to be is anybody's guess -- whitest tints to yellow, with emerald, olive and dark green, with countless hues in between. The hillsides are decked out and rocks and trees besides, with leaves and lichen, and the softest moss. Taking in spring's glory is enough for me. Who needs to hear chatter at a time like this?

Don't get me wrong. I'm as convivial as the next person. There's nothing like being with friends from time to time, sharing a delicious dinner and good conversation. It's just that I don't feel bereft without this.

Doesn't always having to have people around us, not willing to just be alone with one's own thoughts, bespeak a lack of inner resources? It seems so to me. And just think: it's possible to be in a roomful of people, and yet feel lonely. Conversely, when

we've taken the time, and effort, to develop interests beyond ourselves, we can be all alone humanly speaking, yet not be lonely at all.

Whether it's an interest in great music or literature, or learning a foreign language, or getting involved in some activity that helps our fellow beings, the right sense of solitude need not be solitary.

Tree Stump, Full of Charm

Of your kind, I've seen quite a few. But you, tree stump full of charm, take home the prize. I stumbled upon you on my last trek through the forest ... the air with just the right amount of crispness to it ... hint of wood smoke wafting by -- a day for definitely not staying indoors.

Whence this penchant for wandering in woods and forests, I've often wondered. A person would almost think I had some Native American back there somewhere. There isn't. But it's sure hard not to be outside most of the time. Whether winter, spring, summer or fall, I find an almost unlimited variety of things in nature to ooh and aah over. To me, nature is an essay or poem just waiting to be written.

But back to you, my charming little friend. About three feet high you are, with bright green moss growing here and there. You have English ivy up one side, the cutest toadstools at your base, and weather-sculpted crevices where tiny creatures must love to abide.

Nature is filled with such objects of delight!

You've got personality, kid.

That Face at the Window

One of the best things about coming home, besides loving to be there, is driving up and seeing our doggie's expectant face at the window. No matter how long we're away, she's almost always at her post.

Who but a person's dog could show such devotion. Money couldn't buy such fidelity. And certainly nothing could compel it that we could do or say.

We keep telling her, as do others, with your looks --especially those huge brown eyes -- you'd be a cinch to sell just about anything on TV.

But we don't want her to have to work for a living. We just want her to --

Keep being happy and adorable;

Keep showing that heart-tugging

face at the window.

A Card Come to Life

Some years ago, a friend of ours who still lives in New England sent me a darling card with the cutest kitten on it. This animal was tucked in a pretty bed, reclining on a pretty rose-print pillow. It had the most contented look on its face.

I couldn't throw that card away. Something about it captured me. We didn't have a cat then, even though I had a gorgeous Persian while growing up that I just loved. Being married to a bird-lover plus, cats just didn't seem on my horizon.

Then something wonderful happened. A black kitten wandered into our yard one day. He kept coming around our house, obviously very hungry and homeless. But at first, he was shooed away in favor of the birds. But he didn't give up. We gave in, and started feeding him. Had to work some time to get him tame enough to let us pet him. But then one day, what a thrill when he let me pick him up.

The wonderful thing to me about this is that Mischa looks just like the kitty on that card I kept. He could be its twin. As our friend said, "Doesn't God work in wonderful ways, though,"

Angel Helpers

I do believe we encountered one a couple of years ago when we were in a quandary about a kitten we had just rescued. Mischa came to us one day, hungry, homeless, obviously wild. With two dogs, we initially shooed him away. But he kept coming back around, helping himself to food left out for woodland creatures.

This was in the summer months, and by the time winter approached, it seemed we had no choice but to give him away. He couldn't be in the house, and he wouldn't survive outdoors. Or so we thought. Having grown quite attached to this little fellow -- a beautiful Tuxedo cat, black and white with huge green eyes -- it was a wrench to think of not keeping him.

Then one day my husband and I had gotten out of our car at a store when there before us was a woman with a cat on a leash, of all sights. We struck up a conversation and found out she was on a car trip. We mentioned that we had a cat but probably wouldn't get to keep him, what with winter coming on.

What she said was surprising, but so comforting. She said being from Maine, she knew cats that could survive all winter outdoors. "Not to worry.", she said. "Just put your cat in the garage on fluffy blankets, if you wish, and he'll be fine."

We thanked her with such a feeling of relief. Why, we can keep Mischa, we said! I have since felt that this woman was an angel helper God caused to appear to us in a form that would meet our immediate need. And so it did. (Mischa has since joined the household--the dogs becoming acclimated to him--and he sleeps indoors, happily.)

What Joy Can Do

We had seen this jogger before, a college girl she seemed, on the path where we often walk our dogs.

But this particular morning, unlike the couple of other times of running on past us, she doubled back and stopped. "You don't know what your happy faces do for me!", she said. Total surprise on our part. And more. A feeling of "Who, us?" -- not one word of cheer having passed our lips, not knowing that this girl needed to see smiling faces.

It isn't easy to feel cheery these days, I realize --probably any days -- what with all the gloom-producing things going on in the world. Some friends of ours have even given up on watching news reports, so grim are the stories. So, I suppose the tiniest expression of happiness on our part can help lift another person's spirits, and do more good for our fellow beings than we may think.

Therefore, point taken: resolved to cultivate joy. Not paste it on.

But *feel* it.

Show it.

Going Through the Doggie-Rub Machine

Dogs can do the cutest things. How our little Beagle thought up something she likes to do each evening, what we have termed going through the doggie-rub machine, (something like going through a car wash) we'll never know. But it gets her even more attention. I don't know if most other breeds of dogs require constant affirmation that they're still loved and wanted, but Sasha certainly does.

When we're watching TV, with our feet up on an old coffee table that can't look worse than it already does, here comes our little doggie under. She pauses just so, so that my husband pets her at one end, and I get to work on her ears.

We don't mind, given the way she started out life, apparently quite abused. Abused to the point that her former owners, they think, just left her by the side of the highway one day. But some kind souls at the Oak Ridge, Tennessee Humane Society picked her up and brought her over to our town to a pet store where we adopted her.

She's so happy today. And so are we to have such a delightful little dog.

You Don't Have to be a Kid Again ...

. . . to love a teddy bear. Or two, in our case. While my husband and I had them as children no doubt, we happen to still have teddy bears.

To go back a bit, we've had them since Christmas 1986 where they were bought in Boston, Massachusetts. They're Russian brown bears, perfectly beautiful, and they were shipped from Korea where we lived for a time. My husband had a special assignment in Seoul and we came to love the people there and their country. So it was fun to think of teddy bears from Seoul.

We decided to give them names--Feelix and Feelicia. A boy for him, and a girl for me. Where these names came from, who knows? But in those years when we traveled so much and had no children, not even a dog or cat to cuddle, we latched onto our bears.

And in a way, they've been a comforting presence in the various homes we've lived in. In the upheaval and uncertainty that come to most families, these teddy bears have brought us solace. They sit side by side on a chest of drawers, and each time we squeeze them (yes, we do), out comes love--years of love. I realize that people look to different constants in their lives to feel a sense of the familiar and for us, it just happened to be these stuffed animals.

So in my humble opinion, whatever makes you feel like a kid again when you are not, go for it. Who's to say it's silly, that you've outgrown such and such? If it's an outlet for affection, delight in it the way a child would.

Our Literary Dog

Being that we're Welsh, when we got our first puppy we decided to name him after a Welshman who is one of our favorite poets. And would you believe, one day Dylan decided to write a poem and send it into our local newspaper. The editor was interested, saying "It isn't often that we get a contribution from the canine part of our population." And he published it, to the delight of many of our neighbors.

Here is our dog's first creative offering about a spot we all visit frequently:

"Disney World for Dogs"

This is my first poem,
And it may be my last,
But since I was named
For Welsh poet, Dylan Thomas,
To go with Howell, which is Welsh,
I want to take advantage of this venue
To send doggie kisses to the folks
Who planned and constructed
The park at the Farragut Public Library.

I extend my paw to the Town fathers;
They did a bang-up job in my view,
And Sasha agrees wholeheartedly.
To think, all we have to do
Is climb in the car,
Go a couple of miles from our house,
Get out and get to have enough fun
For a whole barrel of monkeys--
Climbing over picturesque logs,
Going across lovely bridges,
Wading in rock-strewn streams,
Walking wood-chip paths,
Meeting neighborhood dogs of all kinds.
Get our leashes. We're ready to go again!

Look at Me Now

"You're not thinking of becoming a writer", someone once said to me. "You're not intellectual enough", another wise and published friend offered.

So I didn't try--for too many years. Then one wonderful day unforgettable, writing began to flow. It was as though a spring was bubbling up which I couldn't (and didn't want to) shut off. Writing that has warmed people, made them laugh and weep, inspired them. And in some cases, made them want to amend their lives. Truly.

Take it from me then. Don't ever let anyone convince you to keep your words bottled up. Express what you feel--boldly. That's all there is to style, in my opinion. Isn't what you have to share as valid as anybody else's? So have your say. If it's in your heart, it will reach the hearts of others.

And besides, you have a Companion who will see you through each step of the way. A Companion that will be true, if only you know it. If only you depend upon Him.

Such Cute Little Faces

We loved those raccoons of Willow Gate Rise. (Love the name of our street, though there wasn't a willow tree or gate in sight, and only a slight rise in our long road. The person who chose the name must have been a writer. But no matter.)

Those creatures were so dear. And for many a year, my husband would put food out--even after hefty New England snows and a terrific lot of shoveling to clear their dinner area. Up to the retaining wall they would go, settle down on their bottoms, and feast on the loot. Oh they were so cute! And when baby raccoons came along, a mother would be quite tame. With the need to feed so many mouths, she would seem half starved herself, willing to come up close to us.

Then one day the moving van came, and with a pang we had to leave them behind. Would the new owners follow our instructions and keep these darling things alive? Vain hope, I would think. The couple who bought our house didn't seem to be the animal lovers we were.

We've often wondered how the raccoons got along with us gone. But we tried to realize that their Maker would no doubt find a way to sustain them. Perhaps they would go back to the wild (what there was left, what with ever-increasing housing developments springing up), as they had been doing before we welcomed them into our yard. We had heard somewhere that we shouldn't be feeding wildlife. But my husband was such a birdlover and put out seed for over 15 species of birds that it became necessary to put out something for the raccoons so they wouldn't scarf all the birds' food. That was how it all started, and we

weren't a bit sorry.

I'm happy to report that the joy of seeing these little woodland creatures--foxes, possums, skunks, and rabbits too--continues to this day in our new place here in Tennessee. And every now and then, as it's getting dark, we get to see a cute little raccoon face. And some even come up very close, settle down, and begin to feast.

Is it Storming on Orkney?

I love storms -- especially being out in them. Not storms that bring destruction to people and their loved ones, of course. But to feel nature in its element, so to speak. To experience the sensation of wind and rain on my face is something I can't get enough of.

And where I would most like to be when it's storming? In the Orkney Islands, Scotland. Not that I've ever been there, but a photo I once saw has excited my imagination and stayed with me.

There was the most quaint little dwelling, perched not far from the sea (which one, I don't know), probably the North Sea off Scotland's coast. But the photographer had captured the feel of the raging storm. And I could just imagine myself all snug inside the cottage, under a downy comforter, with a mug of strong tea and perhaps a scone or two. And a good book, waiting out the storm. Not that I wouldn't have spent some time walking along that coast,with the wind and rain pelting me.

Not all folks incline toward Scottish weather, I have read. It's far too rough for most. But not for me. And one of these days, I intend to visit the Orkney Islands, and hope that I encounter one of its storms.

I can't wait!

Companions True

I believe nothing one can do can repay a dog's devotion, nor bring that emotion of being uniquely cared for.

There was this one day when feeling quite ill, I was flopped across our bed. At once our big dog came up beside, placed a big paw on my arm, and stayed with me for some time, as if to say, "I understand what you're going through."

What a wonderful thing it is that dogs can feel such empathy for their owners (do not like this word "owners"--for their families who love and take care of them ... there, that's better). Where it comes from, who knows? But that most of our canine companions possess this sensitivity is well documented.

Many are the examples I could cite to the person who has yet to experience the rewards of having such a loving friend. But for those of you who do, you know right away what I'm talking about here.

Back to that particular day, words are inadequate to convey the peculiar comfort our dog's presence brought me. I actually felt better physically. The love being shown was so pure, it left me feeling quite sure that this aided in my recovering. How could I not, with such a faithful companion hovering?

And some people will still say that animals are dumb.

Yeah, right.

Homecoming

I had to give the speech, and modesty aside, it was an honour to be asked. But oh how anxious I was to leave New York City behind, and make my connection in Charlotte, North Carolina. Traveling far and wide? Been there, done that. (At least for the time being.) It was back home where I yearned to be.

I flew out of the terminal at Knoxville, Tennessee and there pausing by the curb were my two favorite guys: one behind the wheel of the car, the other with head and paws hanging out of the window. What joy I felt.

Then another time, we were only fifty miles from home. On our way back from Texas where we had spent Christmas with relatives, I was about as bad as some travelers in the high-energy northeast USA. On one trip, a fellow passenger remarked, "People in Boston try to get off the plane before it's landed!"

After a treacherous ice storm going down, and tricky, slick roads coming back, I could hardly sit still the last few miles. But oh the smiles when we rounded the corner of our street, and our house was still there. Of course, we knew it would be. But isn't coming home just heavenly!

What Keeps us Young

When we got our first dog, people would say, "It will keep you young, looking after a puppy." And I do believe there's something to this. Having an animal to care for does keep one on the go, feeling and acting more youthful, that's for sure.

Why would this be so often the case? I think it's because of the unselfish love these dependent beings get from us. Or at least I hope they all do. Such affection is, in my view, an aspect, a reflection of that Love divine which their Creator has for all His creatures, great and small. A person just doesn't have that much time left over to become self-absorbed.

In addition to keeping one young as he or she forgets about self, a friend once said to me that what got her up each day as she was going through a rough time in her life, was knowing that her dear little dog was counting on her. She had to get up to feed him and take him outdoors. "It was due to this animal that I didn't sink into depression and just shut down from living altogether", she said.

And I can't help thinking, kept her young as well.

Of course, it doesn't have to be a beloved animal that does this for us. Anything we really love to do, anything that fires us up and gets us up in the morning (or keeps us up late at night--whatever) will do the job. Whether it's a job we love going to, a volunteer project of some kind, or some outlet for our creativity, knowing we're doing something of use to someone, or to the world at large, gives us a glow that preoccupation with ourselves just can't give.

The Picture of Innocence

Who can look at a sleeping pet, and not feel his or her heart tug? Some poor soul who needs to feel love a lot more, in my view. A person whose soul needs to be awakened, that's who.

Is there anything more stirring to look at (to a lover of animals) than one's beloved pet in repose? I suppose there may be. Perhaps to a parent gazing at their sleeping child. About this I wouldn't know.

I say to our doggie, you are sometimes challenging when awake, like when we have a terrific thunder and lightning storm. Or when fireworks go off. You were as a puppy sometimes wild, more than once slipping out of your harness, and giving us a chase through wooded areas almost too dense to navigate. Anxious times these were, but you always stopped long enough for us to get you secured once again.

But now when you're asleep on bed or rug or floor, your innocence moves us to the core.

With us Everywhere

"God is with you in everything you do"* -- words so very true, words meant for me and you. They're on a bookmark a dear friend sent me from afar, and I see this little gift in a book I read almost every day.

Whether it's day or night, whether we're at home or far away, whether we're feeling up and cheery, or downhearted and weary, what a faith-lighted thought this is, that our loving Father is never apart from us.

Is this not glorious to think about? That His care does surround us; His loving arms are always around us. Not only us, but those we love--beside them always, above. And not only those we're close to, and friends we greet, but people on the other side of the world we probably will never meet.

What would mankind do if these words were not true? But oh they are ... something circumstances which we may encounter cannot erase.

God with us -- what a treasure, a comforting presence without measure.

*See Genesis 21 :22

Winter Postcard

The hill was covered with sparkling snow, fresh, fallen just that day ... pristine but for one set of footprints which to the top made their way. What was it about this winter scene that made me stop and stare?

It was recalling a feeling from childhood, peering through the window and seeing the year's first snowfall, everything so soft and still and beautiful. Standing there on that day on the sidewalk I felt a little girl's sheer joy in living come magically over me again. What joy it was great to be out in the cold, clean winter air.

Not that I'd ever want to live up North again. Too much snow-shoveling required. By the home owner's usually, when there's just been a blizzard and commercial plowers are nowhere to be seen.

No, I prefer the snows we have down here in the South. Just enough to make the landscape lovely, just enough to play in, just enough to clear away without too much effort.

And just enough snow covering the hills to slide down.

The Cat Who doesn't Know He's Not a Dog

In all our years of married life, we never had a cat so didn't know quite what to expect. But it seems we have one who, in many respects, is more like a dog than a cat.

Mischa comes when called. He actually does. And he takes walks with us when we got out with Dylan and Sasha. He really does this, too. Neighbors have remarked on this sight, and one friend who is a big cat-person and knows much about felines said, "That's a cat who doesn't know he's not a dog."

Not long ago, my husband had to deliver something to a neighbor three doors down, and as he walked up the street, our cat followed right behind. There is a long driveway, and as John went up that, and across the walk to the front door, there was Mischa following closely behind. Not only this, he kept in step all the way back to our house.

A most remarkable cat we do have.

When We're up Against it

Not long ago we happened to see a program on World War II, on the Pacific campaign. The battle of Iwo Jima, to be exact. Although I knew about the fierce fighting that went on there due to a close friend of my mother's who served in the Marines and shared some of his experience, something new came to light. The narrator said that 1 out 3 Marines was either killed or wounded. 1 out of 3!

I couldn't help thinking about Frank who came through that murderous conflict with not a scratch. Many pounds thinner, but this was all. And to what did this boy (which he was, only 18) owe his deliverance? To the conviction he had gained from studying Christian Science that God was always with him. He was in fact a student in the Sunday School at the time of his enlistment, and what he had learned there brought him through intact, he said.

And the other WWII experience involved a friend of ours in Australia. Paul served in the Solomon Islands and was also a lifelong student of Christian Science. To what did he owe his safety through months of intense jungle fighting? It was this, he once told me. I knew that "God and I are not two, but one; and that one is God."

Where did this concept of God's ever-presence come from? He said it was primarily this statement from *Science and Health with Key to the Scriptures* by Mary Baker Eddy: "Jesus of Nazareth taught and demonstrated man's oneness with God, and for this we owe him endless homage." (page 18)

As these two friends proved, when we feel up against it and

the situation appears dire, one who trusts in God's care who as the Bible assures us time and time again, is an ever-present, unfailing help in trouble, can come through unscathed.

It is obvious that Christ Jesus fully realized the inseparability of man from God. He taught that man is God's own child, safe in the care and love of his Creator, regardless of appearances. I've thought often of the time when our Master was in a crowd. Some of the people intended to throw him off a hill. And yet, we read that he passed through the midst of them, totally untouched.

The Psalmist sang, "Lord, thou hast been our dwelling place in all generations." (Ps 90: 1) It is for this reason that in truth we are eternally exempt from harm of any kind. I like to think about this: we have actually never been apart from our divine source, God--not even for a moment. As His offspring, dwelling in Him, we are and have always been preserved by His unerring laws of order, safety and exemption from dangerous conditions. What a potent help this is in everyday life, I have found many times.

Frank, who was highly decorated but wouldn't own up to his heroism if placed before a firing squad, actually lives near us. In Oak Ridge, Tennessee whom we see from time to time. And Paul, who has passed on, has left us a lovely reminder of his friendship. Atop a bookcase is a platypus he carved himself out of rare Tasmanian wood. And we have his poetry. I feel sure Paul is creating still, life for him and others made even more fruitful by that unseen *felt* Presence so many God-trusting individuals know.

Dogs and Their Stuffed Toys

Is there a more adorable sight than a puppy carrying some cute toy around the house? Our little Beagle does this all the time. When someone comes to the door that she knows, she runs into the family room, selects some stuffed animal and greets the person. She does this when we come back, in a doggie way, celebrating that we're home.

When she comes upstairs in the afternoon for a nap, she selects some friends to sleep with her. What determines which animal--moose, rabbit, frog, chipmunk, wolf, hedgehog or some other--she takes, is anyone's guess. But they must mean something to her. Sometimes she will help us out by carrying one back downstairs when it's time to eat. But we often have an armful of these creatures.

And one of the fondest memories we have of visiting my husband's aunt in Austin, Texas is getting to play with Mr. Kerby, her Springer Spaniel. We didn't have a dog of our own then, as we traveled a lot in our work. So, it was a special treat to have one right at hand for several days. In fact, one day at lunch, Martha Frances said after observing our joy in playing with her dog, "You are two people who need to get a dog."

She and her husband were high up in the oil business, and would have some pretty ritzy visitors from all over world. And no matter how classy they were (and some were royal), they would have to get used to this dog waking them up each morning. In fact, Mr. Kerby would gently push open the door to the guest room and come up to their side of the bed. They would hear a soft breathing

43

or sense something nearby. And then, they would see this dog with his stuffed animal of the day in his mouth. It was a custom with him to pick one or the other, but his favorite seemed to be a nearly worn-out pink piggy.

Most were charmed by this display, but probably not all. But as for me and my husband, we loved being greeted by this adorable dog and his stuffed toys.

Just Be in By Dark

Our little cat, before we took him in, was a wild thing, accustomed to going where he wanted, when he wanted. Obviously so, since he had no home, no one to care what happened to him. He has become, over the almost three years we've been fortunate enough to have him to look after, much more domesticated. But being a boy cat (he was fixed which stopped a lot of the fighting he used to do) he still roams about in the daytime as he appears to have quite a territory to check out.

More than once, as darkness was coming on, we began to get a bit anxious for him to get in soon. If Mischa didn't show up when I called (yes, he does come when called usually--much like a dog which has surprised us), after some time I would go out into our neighborhood, looking for him. But thank God, whom we like to think is ultimately the One who looks after him, this family member has always showed up. Nonchalantly so, but there he was, safe and sound. Perhaps he had been under a bush somewhere, not ready to come in, just ignoring my calls, which I understand cats sometimes do.

But every time we let him out, we always say, wander (mostly) where you wish. But just be in my dark.

Movin' On

I don't know about you, but speaking for myself, when friendships change, there's no use in hanging on -- and I'm talking about someone clinging to me. Just do not like people draped around my shoulders, as it were -- wanting things to remain static, rooted in a musty past. After all, no one owns us, do they?

As some friends of Samuel Johnson once said when they came to him where he was dining, "Sir, we have a claim on you." Whereupon the great thinker and writer replied, "You MAY think that," and went right on doing what he wanted to, paying no heed to their wishes to hold him back.

"But isn't being as independent as you describe rather cold?" you may be thinking about now. No, it isn't. Not to me. There is nothing like being together, yet apart, I have found. Much like two trees growing close together but not leaning on one another, someone has said. This is the way it is with those relationships I cherish.

If someone truly cares about us and our well-being, wouldn't they be willing to leave us room to develop and become what we are meant to be? I think so. And if they're not, it may be an indication that they're thinking from a selfish standpoint. As with those friends of Samuel Johnson, they were probably thinking more about not losing his enriching companionship more than they were interested in whatever new ventures he had in mind.

In my view of the situation, autonomy and kindheartedness are in no way incompatible. Having the courage to express both

(and it does take courage I am discovering) has disentangled me from alliances outgrown; removed me from places where I no longer needed to be. When it's time to move on, we need to move on.

Yes sir, to me there's nothing like having the right amount of freedom. Just can't imagine life any other way.

Dotting the "i", Crossing the "t"

Can anything that can (and does) come up in our day to day experience baffle the Creator of all? No, I sincerely believe. He can clear the way--whatever the thicket appears to be.

God can bring to light solutions that we, unaided, just cannot see. The Old Testament says, "In all thy ways acknowledge him, and he shall direct thy paths." Besides doing what an obedient child of His should be doing, it makes sense to me to be turning ever more to the One divine Mind for help.

More than once lately when we've faced a serious glitch and had no idea what to do, God showed us a solution that I'm sure we would never have thought of. So thorough was the resolution, it was like someone dotting the "i" and crossing the "t", so to speak.

I recall some years ago when a business situation had me in a tight corner. I happened to mention it to a close and wise friend. "Whom can I take this problem to?" I asked him. "Why not take it to God?", my friend suggested. At that stage in my spiritual growth, this seemed like a radical step. But the friend was on the right track. And instead of turning to people so much, I've learned that superior -- and quicker -- answers come when we acknowledge God's wisdom. And trust in it.

So, while I'm writing this essay primarily to praise and honour You, thank You for all the things you do.

48

Humble Yet Strong

Sometimes daughters of the South are too sweet and light. They lack might, are reluctant to fight when the Cause is right.

Acting humble, while standing up for oneself -- what a challenge this can be. After centuries of half the race being put down, being told to be seen and not heard (with a few exceptions) can make one want to go overboard in expressing oneself. Sometimes it's tough keeping the rejoinders in, hard to not commit the sin of being unloving to our fellow beings.

But there's our Hero for all time, our Exemplar sublime, who though his rebuke was something one would not have wanted to be on the receiving end of, was the most loving man that ever walked the earth. And the most humble.

Somewhere I have read that the 3 most important things in the Christian life are humility, humility, and humility. There's no denying that this is a winsome quality. And it may that in emulating Jesus in this way, we become stronger as well.

Being daughters (and sons) of the King, shouldn't we be able to express humility and strength? This we followers of Christ will increasingly need to do, I do believe.

Retirement? Never!

The woman sitting down the bench from me that day told me she had just retired. "I don't know what to do all day. There's not enough to fill the hours", she lamented. An air of boredom, almost dejection, hovered over her. How very sad, I thought.

Although decades away from so-called retirement myself, something about this woman made me think. "I'm never going to give up an active life", I vowed. And I haven't.

With so much to learn and see and do in life, why shut ourselves down? As Arthur Fiedler, the long-time conductor of the Boston Pops Orchestra once said in an interview, "He who rests, rots." And Albert Schweitzer wrote: "The great secret of success is to go through life as a man who never gets used up." Both these pieces of advice from men who led a very productive life in their later years have stayed with me.

After all, age is so mental, don't you think? I've known individuals who were quite young in years who already had an aspect about them of being out to pasture, so to speak. And conversely, those inspiring men and women who not only acted youthful; they looked that way. How could they not, given their lives of meaningful activity and usefulness to their communities and often the whole world? .

When it comes to the subject of retirement, one finds divided feelings--some for, some vehemently against. To one person, retirement conveys the picture of long-awaited leisure; to another, the dread of enforced idleness, unhappiness, and loss of purpose.

But whether one's personal preference is for a rest or for continued activity, he could scarcely look forward to experiencing what the dictionary says about "retire", which is, in part, to "retreat", "recede", or "withdraw."

My view of this is that while withdrawing from certain human commitments does provide a welcome change in one's lifestyle, we don't have to leave behind a sense of purpose. Without this sense of having some contribution to make, can all the travel, excitement, social diversion, and hobbies in the world fill the void?

It isn't only the person who is retiring from business after decades of service who faces the lurking foe of uselessness. This challenge also cuts into that segment of society composed of younger people. For example, veterans back from current engagements in the military can feel retired even though they have yet to begin their life's work.

And housewives who have not spent one day within the walls of business can feel a haunting emptiness. They may find that wanting to be a conscientious wife and mother does not alone bring the total fulfillment they were educated to expect. And this can sometimes almost make them feel retired against their will. Some think the solution is to go out and get a job. But then they learn that just as many office workers experience the same discontent. No, something more is needed.

When the feeling of "What am I really living for?" overtakes one, this may be an indication that he is actually ready to think about helping others, doing some good in the world, forgetting about self so much. And goodness knows, the opportunities that lie down this road are vast, for a person who is mentally and physically able to be up and doing. There's no dearth of

humanitarian work that desperately needs all the help it can get.

It isn't uncommon for advanced thinkers who have grasped the importance of making a difference to mankind to continue in a useful, satisfying enterprise for years. And they often find a completely new line of endeavor. Their lives prove that it is never too late for one who understands that he has talents that could be being put to good use for the welfare of others.

So, here's to being more childlike--not childish or silly, for heaven's sake--but maintaining one's sense of wonder, adventure, excitement, expectancy. With the right mental attitude, one can look forward to ever-expanding horizons, with plenty to live for.

Sordid, Senseless, Self-indulgence

One doesn't have to be a reader of the tabloids to know what has been happening in the world with altogether too much frequency. There are too many people whose lives are being upended by mindless self-indulgence.

Thinking about what walking the broad way of worldliness can do to someone, not to mention their families, can't help but reflect on the teachings of Christ Jesus vis-a-vis the 2 paths that are open to us in this life: the one that leads to destruction, and the other that seems to many to be difficult and un-appetizing to take, but that leads to all worth having -- now and eternally.

In the words of our Master, "Enter ye in at the strait gate: for wide is the gate, and broad is the way, that leadeth to destruction, and many there be which go in thereat;
Because strait is the gate, and narrow is the way, which leadeth unto life, and few there be that find it." This is from the New Testament, as many will recognize.

Jesus isn't saying that one is doomed if he has chosen unwisely, just that there seem to be few who are willing to exercise the self-denial it takes to choose the better way. One should make every effort to ensure that he's among the "few".

God be thanked for His infinite love and mercy, that now is not too soon to start getting one's heart right with God. Nor is it too late to retrace one's steps, if he (or she) has wandered off the path through deplorable living for one's own self-gratification.

Be serious about doing what Jesus commands. He is a
Companion true, and your heavenly Father wants you to be safe
with Him. It is the one sure,

the royal,

the only way.

A Few Kind Words

Who can estimate the good we can do when we take a little time out to notice what others are about; to show some appreciation; to offer some encouragement. A life can be turned around, inspired thought unsealed, latent talent revealed, with a few kind words.

I know whereof I speak. Beginning to write, with publication nowhere in sight, someone who was a professional writer went out of his way one fine day, to say: "Keep at your writing. I see something in it. Just persevere." That man, what a dear! It meant the world to me at that time that there was actually someone who saw promise in my manuscripts.

And from time to time, when I run across someone who is obviously alive to life, a sensitive soul who feels things deeply, I ask them; "Do you write, or paint, or do something else of a creative nature?" And just the other day, I put this question to a very nice young man who serves me at a favorite restaurant. His face brightened and he said: "Oh, I'd love to write! There's so much I want to say. But I don't know how to get started." To which I replied, "You've got to get the words down on paper. Or on a computer. Then you'll have something to work with. I'm sure you have something to share with the world." I left thinking that this man was encouraged to try since someone took the time to listen to him and to show a little interest.

So, you never know, this aspiring writer may just end up writing a book someday -- all because of a few kind words.